TRUE STORIES OF HOW PRINCE CHANGED PEOPLE'S LIVES

Patia Adonis

authorHOUSE®

AuthorHouse™
1663 Liberty Drive
Bloomington, IN 47403
www.authorhouse.com
Phone: 1 (800) 839-8640

Published by AuthorHouse 03/24/2018

ISBN: 978-1-5462-3357-2 (sc)
ISBN: 978-1-5462-3356-5 (e)

Print information available on the last page.

This book is printed on acid-free paper.

Thank you to my husband for his unwavering love and support. To my children, always follow your heart, you never know where it will take you. And to Prince...thank you will never be enough. You are with us every day.

INTRODUCTION

As the cold wind blew my car and Diamonds and Pearls blared, I drove to the one and only Paisley Park in December of 2016. The place that filled so many of our hearts and intrigued our minds was now open to the public. My journey had been a long one, driving over 700 miles in the dead of winter with my family. I cannot tell you why I made the journey, besides I had a gut feeling that I needed to go. I wish I had the story of seeing him in multiple concerts and his songs being the sound track of my life, but that was not my story. Being a music fanatic for as long as I can remember, I knew Prince was one of a kind and such an interesting artist, but when he passed away something changed for me. I felt a horrible sense of guilt for not following him when he was alive. I was devastated that I missed the Prince experience, and later

I found out that I was even more devastated that I missed Prince the friend, activist and artist. All of this propelled me to make my first trip to Minneapolis.

As I pulled up to the large white almost commercial like Paisley Park, I couldn't believe my eyes. I was sitting at Paisley Park. I never thought in a million years that I would be sitting there. As I entered and the warm smell of lavender floated through the air while Prince's music softly played in the background; I could see why this was Prince's sanctuary. It drew you in; I knew right then and there I did not want to leave. Starting the tour and seeing his legendary telecaster with animal print strap, then seeing his urn to the other side would bring anyone to their knees. Sadness filled my soul, yet gratitude to this man filled my heart. Gratitude of everything he had given us while he is alive. The tour continued, and being in Prince's world where he created his masterpieces was surreal. As the tour came to an end, I couldn't help but to tear up. Watching his super bowl performance as he sang Purple Rain while standing in his home was simply too much to handle. I walked aimlessly through the gift shop. Knowing I would have to leave, but not wanting to. I finally peeled myself out of the building. I drove across the street to Caribou Coffee and sat in the parking lot. Looking across the road towards Paisley Park, I stared at the roads where Prince once rode his bike. It all of a sudden became bitterly clear that Prince was gone. I then could not but help to think, "Why am I here? Why did I drag my husband and two small kids to Minneapolis?

What am I looking for?" I drove back to our hotel and was greeted by my excited kids who wanted to go swim at the hotel pool. The rest of our time in Minneapolis was great, but I left almost more confused than ever.

Shortly after returning home I started spending more time on Instagram. I had started a Prince Instagram page (_princenation_) a few months earlier to share pictures and to learn more about Prince. I started reaching out to others and reading anything I could get my hands on regarding Prince. That is when life began to change. I started reading and hearing stories; stories of Prince's quiet generosity, of how he inspired people and how he changed people's lives. The more I spoke with people from around the world, the more I knew these stories were meant to be shared. Inspirational, sad, funny, happy...it did not matter. Prince changed people forever. It became very clear to me, if I hadn't made the trip to Paisley Park I would have not reached out to others. The reason for my trip was to write this book. My hope for this book is that it will reach people who never thought twice about Prince. Maybe it will send them on their own journey to Minneapolis or to pick up a Prince record. I also hope this will make the purple army smile and to think about their own stories. The following stories were written by people who volunteered their writing for this book. The stories are from all over the world, every gender, and different ages. Prince reached so many of us. I hope you enjoy these stories as I have...

CHAPTER 1

Vaughan's Story

I feel very lucky to have contacted Vaughan. I know this was not the easiest thing for Vaughan to write, but I thank him. His story is one of my favorites, starting at a young age to now. Enjoy Vaughan's story written by Vaughan himself.

1983, PLYMOUTH, DEVON, UK

I am a 12-year-old boy in Plymouth, shopping with my parents. For some reason I find myself in a record store. I hear this really funky beat and am instantly drawn to it. I have no idea what or who it is, but I like it, I like it a lot. Not being the most confident boy, I pluck up courage to ask who the band are. It is Prince I am told, Prince I think, who is that. I buy the album on tape and when I get home I fast forward it to the song I heard. WOW. It is even better than in the shop. Then that infamous line about fucking the taste out of Marsha's mouth. I loved it and I knew my parents would hate it, but for once I just didn't care. I loved his voice, how he looked, his fashion, the make up and because of Let's Pretend We're Married, so began my love affair with him.

It has been almost two years (as I write this) since he left us, and I still feel a sense of emptiness. Prince was not just an unbelievable musician, he was a genius. Every album seemed to be released at just the right time for me, always a song or lyric (usually a few) that related to my life at that time. I have always been someone who likes his own company, mainly because nobody 'got me'. Prince was like a friend, he got me through the times when I felt lonely, he made things seem ok, like a guiding light. I got so much stick at school for liking him, almost bullied, called gay, faggot etc. Living in a small town of about 4,000, you stood out for liking something different and to all my school mates, he was different. Even my dad questioned my sexuality because I had a huge poster of a half-naked Prince on my bedroom wall. But I just didn't care. I defended him, and his music just took me to places nobody got. Then one night in 86, I was at a party where some of the 'cool' gang from the year above put on the Parade album, obviously their choice was Kiss, a song I still don't really care for. When it finished, I skipped the album to Mountains, then Girls and Boys and finally Anotherloverholenyohead. Suddenly I was accepted for liking Prince, albeit only for a few hours, but I was asked how I knew those tracks, I just said, I have all the albums released so far.

88'

Lovesexy shows were announced. I asked my parents if it was ok for me to go, to be firmly told no. I was gutted but wasn't going to let them stop me. I arranged to stay at a friends at the beginning of August, only to travel to London with a friend's brother to see Lovesexy. That night was just amazing. I only told my parents about it about 10 years ago, but I knew way back then, that nothing would get in the way of Prince. That night was the first of my 30 times seeing him live. Prince has just about got me through every part of my life. The good, the bad and the downright awful, from the birth of my children (my second daughter was born when The Most Beautiful Girl in The World was number one in the UK) through my first marriage breaking up, the ensuing bad times and every major event from there. Every time I saw him live, was a massive Purple high for me, but the comedown was just awful. For weeks I would crave him again. His residency at the O2 in London gave me the chance to really get that high I craved from him. I travelled from Devon 8 times to see him, and even 'met' him at an after show in the Indigo club. He had just done 2.5 hours in the main arena and anticipation was high that he would do the after show. Just before midnight, his band started jamming, I was super excited, Prince in a small venue was what we Prince fams craved. I had been lucky enough to have seen an after-show years before, so this one was long overdue. A door opened to my left, I look and then had to look again. Two bodyguards were stood right next to me, with Prince a mere 3 feet from me. I couldn't speak, here was my idol stood within feet of me, looking straight at me and smiling. My mouth was moving but nothing was coming out. All I could do was spin my wife around and point. He laughed, I was like a goldfish and then as if by magic he was gone and on stage. Almost 4 hours later, we were leaving the club, mind blown. The GREATEST NIGHT OF MY LIFE. I managed to take my eldest two daughters to the O2 to see him. My eldest cried through Purple Rain, as I did every time. She turned to her sister and I heard her say. OMG, we are only seeing Prince. As we left the arena, she looked at me and said, Dad, I can see why you love Prince so much, I do too now. Her education was complete. I have seen some amazing Prince shows over the years, from my first at Lovesexy, Nude, Diamonds and Pearls, Live experience, Act II, O2 residency, Hit N Run (Manc Academy 2nd night) Hit N Run 2, Malahide Castle, where it actually started raining during Purple Rain and promptly stopped as it ended, and my 30th and final one which was a 'secret' although a badly kept one in the Prince community, at Koko in Camden, London. The whole day was awesome. Meeting fellow Prince fans is always good, and for those few hours when you are together, you belong to something magical.

April 21st 2016

The day I had always dreaded had come. I had said a few days before that I feared 2016 was the year we would lose him. A fellow fan and I had been worried about his health since the Hit N Run gigs in 2014. I really didn't expect it to be so soon though and that day will live with me forever. I sat numb and speechless as the news broke over social media and the news channels and then I cried and cried and cried for days. My one constant over the past 33 years was gone. My friend, my escape, my passion was taken just like that. It was like a huge part of me had died. My non-Prince friends, just don't get it they laughed at me for being upset. They are no longer my friends. But, do you know what? They were so much poorer for not getting him, for not witnessing his genius live, for hearing all those unbelievably amazing songs that were never singles, having those Purple highs we all craved and had. I am so glad I was alive when he was, to witness a human being that will never be matched. He was a gift to the world and I am thankful I 'got it'. To quote him. All good things they say, never last. But he continues to influence me, and I loved him and always will.

Vaughan Wood, United Kingdom

CHAPTER 2

Linda's Story

What I love about Linda, is she stands up for what she believes in. Her love for animals and equality reminded me so much of Prince. I hope you enjoy her story, written in her own words.

As I sit and write this, it is raining. Maybe a sign for the guidance that I just requested from him, to help me "speak" from the heart.

I first fell under the spell of Prince during the "Purple Rain" era. I mean, who didn't take notice and become an instant fan? After hearing the tracks of "Purple Rain", "Let's Go Crazy", "Baby I'm A Star" and one of my all-time favorites "When Doves Cry", I was hooked! My friend, Jim, and I would hang out and listen to this amazing album. And on weekends we'd hit a little bar in town called "Babe & Eddie's", which had a dance floor in the back room. In that back room, is where you'd find me and Jim just feeling the music and making up our own dances, whenever Prince was playing. Sometimes we were the only two on the dance floor, while others sat at surrounding tables. I can be a bit reserved, until I start to feel comfortable with my surroundings, but when Prince was playing, NOTHING could keep me off that dance floor! I could feel his music pumping through my veins. Prince could bring me out of my shell, and that was something I had never experienced before. Those early days were some of the best memories I have, and I will forever treasure them.

As life went on, I got married, had my daughter and got busy with "life". I'd lost my connection to those early days. I missed out on a lot of his incredible music, that I would later discover. And what I mean by "later", was the very devastating day of April 21, 2016, a day the world will never forget. I remember receiving a text from my daughter, that Prince had died. I was completely stunned and in a state of disbelief, that is, until I turned the TV on and it was EVERYWHERE! My heart just sank. I still to this day have moments of disbelief. Needless to say, I searched for anything and everything "Prince", just something to hold onto to try to comfort my aching soul. It was in those days, weeks and months that I discovered all that I had missed over the years. I reconnected to his music, his energy, his message and "him", at a much deeper level than in the early days. I started to see him beyond his music. I found myself gravitating toward his spirituality and his philanthropy, those qualities deeply resonated within my soul. This multi-talented, internationally known superstar gave the world so much of himself, he didn't just stop at the music. He opened minds and hearts, HE CHANGED LIVES, and I believe he continues to do so. He lead by example. He often spoke of his love for God and love for one another. I refer to Prince as one of "God's truest masterpiece's".

How blessed I feel to have lived during his lifetime. How heartbroken I feel to know his earthly presence is no longer here. For me personally, no other artist will ever touch me like Prince has. When he passed, it felt like I'd lost a loved one, and it still does....

May God bless our beautiful Prince, and keep him in perfect peace.
"THANK YOU, Prince"....

Linda Carfagno, New Jersey

CHAPTER 3

Yvonne's Story

When I first spoke with Yvonne, the joy she had when talking about Prince was contagious. It made me wish I could go back in time and ride with her to his concerts. I hope you enjoy Yvonne's story.

My Prince journey began back in 1980, I was 15 years old. My parents were getting a divorce, I wasn't doing well in school and I had started breaking out with cystic acne on my face—all of which destroyed my confidence. When I first discovered Prince, his whimsical and captivating lyrics put to his funky "sound" grabbed a hold of my soul and never let it go. His music made me feel free, beautiful and understood when I needed it the most. I appreciated his authenticity and love for God.

March, 1985, I saw Prince and the Revolution for the first time in San Francisco. My best friend, Nusrat gave me her ticket so I could go in her place with her brother—the show was amazing! From then on, any chance I got to see Prince, I did. Shortly after I turned 21 I moved from San Jose, California to Reno, Nevada. My mom was planning a trip to see me. While she was in transit I found out Prince was playing a show in Oakland during the same time. When she arrived, I explained that I had to go, I wouldn't be able to think of anything else! I skipped out on my mom and got on a bus to Oakland! Still not sure if she has forgotten or forgiven me for that one.

I was at work the morning of Princes passing. "Raspberry Beret" was playing over the speakers. As a co-worker passed by I pointed up with a grin and declared "you know I'm his biggest fan!" Moments later, I heard the devastating news, I refused to believe it. I was profoundly sad, I shared with the rest of the purple world, deep loss and sorrow.

Nusrat has not only been my greatest friend of all time but has shared in my devotion to Prince. In August of 2017 Nusrat and I met in Minneapolis and planned our "Purple Adventure." The morning of our drive to Chanhassen, there was a slight mist in the air, it felt peaceful. We turned left onto Audobon road and there stood the enormous, creative haven, Paisley Park! The atrium was open with clouds and doves on the wall. The tall glass ceiling was bursting with light, I felt his majestic welcome. Each turn and every corner represented his musical genius. From the purple velvet couches to the ping pong and pancakes; the park was truly a magical place. We continued our journey in and around the city. I quickly realized his essence was everywhere. Thank you to the hostess at the Dakota jazz club who let us have a quick peak at the table he used to sit at. The young lady at the caribou who shared a memory of Prince ordering mocha hot chocolate and riding his bike in the parking lot. Every step led us to discover that Prince was truly loved and respected. By the end of our trip it had started raining. I left Minneapolis feeling inspired and fortunate to have had Prince in the background of my life all these years. Thank u Prince.

Yvonne Garcia, Nevada

CHAPTER 4

Kathy's Story

Kathy is truly a ray of sunshine. Her upbeat posts on Instagram and love for Prince is prevalent. Her kindness to others is so apparent. Thank you, Kathy for opening up and letting us know your Prince journey. Here is Kathy's story written in her own words.

What a difference a year can make. So much can change and turn our life around.

When I first heard of Prince's untimely death on April 21, 2016 I was in complete shock and disbelief.

His death had a huge impact on me, not quite understanding why since I hadn't been following his career for years. Marriage and raising a family took precedents to that.

Little did I know my world was about to change in a big way. His transition was going to be the start of my own spiritual growth within. Gods plan for me was about to unfold in the most unexpected way.

At the time of Prince's death I was in the process of trying to come to terms with the end of an 18 year marriage, not by choice. Then I was lead to believe that there would be a reconciliation only to find after months that I was betrayed and lied to, that it was only for monetary gain on my ex-husbands part, sad but true. When someone you spent a huge part of your life loving, putting all your trust, and faith into them to only turn around and find you have been deceived in the most unforgiving way does something to your spirit while knocking you down to your knees. I found myself in a very dark place, feeling hopeless, faithless, and with no purpose in my life, my soul was dead.

For some reason I felt this compelling need to find out what Prince had been up to all these years, so I began to research and look up interviews and videos on him. I was in complete amazement with how much he had done musically over the years, not to mention all his humanitarian work that he chose to keep anonymous.

It was his 1999 interview with Larry King that captured my attention, changing it all for me. I had no idea how spiritual Prince was. Listening to him Praise God for his gift left me in awe, how well spoken he was and full of wisdom. It made me look deep within, it was the beginning of my own spiritual awakening. As he spoke about his well chronicled dispute with WB and ownership of his music, what really had an impact on me was when he said "I really searched deep within to find out the answer to whether fame was most important to me or my spiritual well being and I chose the latter" Wow! it was not about fame or money it was about spiritual wellness.

I realized just as Prince stated his journey was God inspired an inner calling from God, it gave me the courage to face my own despair and give it to God, to be completely dependent on him to guide me to look for my own inner calling.

I began listening to his music non stop everyday, his lyrics were uplifting me and slowly releasing me out of my depression, healing me and giving me a new found purpose. I felt for the first time in a long time that I mattered and I had worth.

That somehow led me to begin my own tribute page within the Purple Family on Instagram and along the way beautiful friendships began unfolding. What a blessing to be a part of the message to spread #love4oneanother and to #lovegod.

I began seeing signs, one that stood out for me were two separate clouds floating across the sky in June of 2016, one was shaped as a guitar and the other as a shoe with a heel..coincidence? I think not..it was that very moment I knew I needed to go to Paisley Park.

In June of 2017 I made that unforgettable life changing journey. To walk through the home of this man who inspired so many through his music, who praised God every opportunity he had, was indeed a great honor. There was no doubt, you could feel his presence it was a healing experience even so much as giving me closure to my own parents that had transitioned.

I left Minneapolis changed on so many levels never to be the same. I had a new found purpose, to inspire others and to give them hope, to believe and have faith that no matter what life throws our way we will get through it. "after every rain, there's a rainbow"

Through this horrible tragedy came hope, a renewed faith for me, my soul awakened not realizing how dormant it had been all these years.

Prince was the light that God lead me to, to trust and believe in love again, he breathed life back into my soul and for that I will eternally be grateful. #Godislove

Thank you Prince Rogers Nelson for sharing yourself with us thorough your music.

But most of all thank you for saving me from that dark place and restoring my faith.

“This thing called life” continues as we your Purple Family lovingly carry your LEGACY forward as we continue to heal.

RIP BEAUTIFUL ONE

Kathy Sarros, Toronto, Canada

CHAPTER 5

Violet's Story

Violet has been such a great teacher to me throughout my Prince experience. Her knowledge of Prince has taught me so much. Her love for Prince and his life is very apparent. Violet is so respectful of his legacy, I am honored for her to be a part of this book.

I was raised in a family of musicians. My parents saw Prince in concert in the late 70's and 80's, and bought every single Warner Bros. release. My first memory of a Prince Song is of Lady Cab Driver. My parents wore that album out well into the late 80s. I literally grew up listening him, and playing piano and bass to his music.

I was blessed to see Prince and the funky-smooth-jazz version of NPG (Rhonda Smith/Bass, Renato Neto/Keys, John Blackwell, Jr/Drums {Rest in Power} plus Hornz) live in Dallas during the Musicology Tour. That tour was so many things to me personally, and to the world at large, changing the way record sales are counted (I still have my CD, it's cracked now, but still plays) and really trumpeting Real Music by Real Musicians.

I took a break from the music scene almost completely (with the exception of listening to classical and inspirational music during study) during law school. I went all in and initially opened my own family law practice. Then, I decided to make some major life changes, moved to a new town, and accepted work that was extremely stressful, and that required excessive travel. I began to go back to live music during off time for stress relief.

The last "new" Prince Song I heard was 1000 X'S and O'S. I'll never forget. I was in my car listening to XM Radio, traveling between courthouses, bobbing my head thinking, daaang, what's that?!? When I looked up and saw his name and the song title I was extremely excited! Right then, I said aloud(and then repeated this statement to family members later that day) "Oh my God, he still sounds so good! That's it. I'm going to see him again next year." Ugh. I feel sick to my stomach every single time I think about it. That was late 2015. Who knew that very next fall I'd be at Paisley, not for a show, but to pay last respects?

Since his passing, I have struggled with the fear that there will not be another even close to who he was in this lifetime, that the true meaning of who he was and what he did will be erased, and the serious question of, "What Now?"

For now, I do my part by traveling for live music. I buy concert tickets for myself and to give to others. I purchase works of art created in various mediums by people who have amazing experiences to share. I visit his museum regularly, and encourage others to do so. I believe that keeping Paisley Park, the Museum of Prince History, and physical monument to all that he accomplished, up and running, for all time, is of the utmost importance. I visit as often as I can and encourage others to do so. I also believe that continuing to show love for his city and the people who helped shape him is paramount. Minneapolis has given us some amazing music, real music by real musicians. Some of the most amazing are still with us jamming all over the city. We need to support.

The people I've met there, all kinds of people, drivers, store owners, people on the street, are just so kind and open, and the vibe is just something different and incredible. Some folks I've met are not even "fans" per se but they're always happy to volunteer a story about their connection to him. There is a purple fire hydrant at Paisley Park that I would never ever in a million years have noticed because...well, just because. Still, the gentleman who sold it came up to me early morning, at a breakfast buffet in Chanhassen, and mentioned it. He said the others are the usual red color but was very excited that they were able to get a purple one for the north fence. He was so proud and excited in sharing his story that I told him I'd make sure to look for it (lol at myself 'looking for the purple fire hydrant'). I did. The gentleman had the cutest little family, wife and two little boys who were fighting to see who got to push the elevator button to a higher floor... That's one thing I love, seeing how far-reaching his effect truly is. There's a certain way people speak when sharing their stories, a certain warmness. They tend to smile more and often want to hug and commiserate - complete strangers of all kinds upon first meeting, just being kind to each other because that's the feeling he generates. So powerful.

He brought so many people together. Those who love him meeting together to be there for each other and celebrate him in this time of grief...well, it's just an amazing thing. I've experienced it, and it's the only thing that helps make the pain somewhat bearable.

He often spoke on supporting Real Musicians/Real Music, ownership of one's creations/ideas, and giving to those in need. Fam should be Willing & Able to do The Work. We should love & take care of one another, the way he asked us to. I still listen to his music, the music of those he inspired, and the music of those inspired by him, daily, because Prince IS Music and Music is Life. Nothing will bring him back, and truly, Nothing Compares to him. We just have to get through this Thing Called Life...*After* the best we can, 2gether.

Violet Brown, Texas

CHAPTER 6

Tia's Story

Words cannot describe how much I appreciate Tia. She was my first friend through Prince and will remain a lifelong friend. Her story is an amazing one, and it was the only way I wanted to end this book. Tia thank you for your honesty and love you have shared. I hope you enjoy her story as much as I have.

Prince came into my life at a very young and tender age. It was at a time after I lost my mother. She was only 38. It didn't take long for me to realize that I was "different" and had been labeled that way because of my situation. There was an isolation I felt that no one could understand because none of my friends had gone through my experience. You see, no other child's parent had died in the little town where I lived. The school didn't know what to do with me, my new placed family didn't know what to do with me, even my friends didn't know what to do with me. So they all just chose not to talk about it. We just didn't talk about her being gone. The emptiness was there. Being a child losing a mother at eleven years old, and then the void began to grow.

I had heard about Prince on the radio as being "weird, eccentric, wild, and different". My first introduction was to the *Prince* album (1979), *Dirty Mind* (1980), and then *Controversy* (1981). I listened to his music and I liked the beat. I didn't understand the words and for years sang to those songs with words that I later came to find were nothing near the actual lyrics. I found myself connecting to the music and this person solely because it seemed like he understood me without even knowing me. I would close my eyes and "feel" the music take me away. Sometimes it felt like I was not even in the same space and time anymore. It was an escape. It was a place of calmness. A place I felt safe. Yet the void continued to grow and I didn't understand why.

The few times I heard Prince speak in an interview, I would take his words and apply them to my life. He didn't care how people viewed him. He made it clear not to let society dictate who you were or who you could be. I held on to those words. It became my mission in life. I was short, a mere 4'10" through most of school and managed to hit 5' by graduation, if my hair was poofed. The album 1999 was kicking and I was moving into different realms of my world. I had been teased all my life because of my thick glasses and height. Somehow through all of the negative backlash I kept pushing forward against the grain believing that there was something in me that was greater. Greater than what I myself couldn't see. It was Prince and his words that kept reeling in my head. Those words like the lyrics in Uptown – "our clothes, our hair, we don't care, it's all about being there". I made it a point to "be there" for people no matter who they were, what they looked like, or how they acted. It shaped me into the person that others would come to and just talk about anything and everything. I became a person that people knew they could trust. The void was rearranging.

I, like many of you, fell deeply in love with Purple Rain; the movie, the music, the enigma, the whole package. In 1984, Prince brought it all together and sucked me right in like a little schoolgirl crush. I think we connected to Purple Rain so intensely because it was easy to find ourselves somewhere in the whole picture of the storyline. For me it was the emptiness I felt in the scenes with his parents. Though there was never any abuse between my parents, I could sense the way Prince portrayed how much he wanted his Father to be proud of him, acknowledge him, and love him. That hit me to my core because those were things I was desperately seeking from my own Father at the time. The void was greater than ever but being replaced with something else. I didn't know what "it" was but I knew things were changing in my soul.

My college years were some of the hardest times in my life. I was trying to understand the "whys" of the world. I felt so empty even though I was surrounded by people who loved me. I always went to church. It was mandatory where I lived. Even in college, I still went to church. I was searching for something and I didn't know what that something was. Prince had become my voice of reason, my lullaby, and my comforter. The music had become my stimulant and my depressant. 1987 *Sign o' the Times* was more prevalent in my life than I wanted to admit to myself. I searched for the words Prince would say in his songs that referenced "God" and "Love". I was looking for direction. I had learned that he would say things similar to 'listen to my music and you'll find who I am'. There was always a meaning behind the lyrics, a message to be read and understood.

For me, it wasn't about Prince the entertainer; it was about Prince the person. He became my go-to. The choices, the decisions, the struggles, I would think about him and his stance on the things of this world and I made better choices because of him. I grew with the music and found a place to go to that felt safe, loving and accepting. This was a place I didn't feel in my world. Prince became that person I could talk to about anything and not worry about him leaving, betraying or not accepting me. He gave me the courage to do things I didn't believe I could do alone and with that courage I graduated from college twice. I had an office administration degree and went back later to receive a respiratory therapist degree.

1995 was a year of change for me. I accepted Christ as my Lord and Savior and only listened to Contemporary Christian music. At that time Prince was in a war with Warner Brothers and his music was laced with strong cursing language and in my opinion showed his anger. I stopped listening to him for a couple of years during that time. It was a strange place for me to be in. Where Prince's music was where I went to for direction, I was now going to Christ. It took some time for me to comprehend that the void I had felt for 16 years was now being filled by Jesus. It was a tug of war. I didn't want to let go of the familiarity of having Prince be that place for me to run to and yet I was feeling a sensation of being free that I had not experienced before. I missed the music. It was confusing and I knew confusion did not come from God so I just stayed back and waited.

Trials came and it was very hard. I was divorced, a single mother and then my boyfriend of 2 years was murdered. I had Jesus. Through these hard times I learned the gift of true forgiveness. I forgave my Father and was able to move forward in my life. I continued to follow Prince via interviews, award shows and guest appearances. I tapped into *Rave Un2 the Joy Fantastic* in 1999 mainly because I loved the look of that era with him wearing his hair long and the glitter and he was in strong force on standing firm to his beliefs regarding owning his masters. This was, of course, what drew me to him from the beginning so hearing him continue to stay consistent in standing on what he believed and fighting for those beliefs kept me respecting him. He never wavered from his stance on the things he believed in no matter how big of a force he was against. Watching his process gave me the encouragement to stand up for myself, and my beliefs, even when they may not have been acceptable to others in my life. By the time *Musicology* came out in 2004, I had morphed into a completely different person. I was stronger, more confident, and certain of who I was and what I was doing with my life. I wasn't running, I was doing.

I was working as a respected Respiratory Therapist and loving life with an adoring husband and great kids. Then in January, 2009, I was hit by a woman who ran a stop sign. I had two major surgeries from that wreck. Eight months later, in September, 2009, I was hit by a 17-year-old drunk driver who ran a red light. This required 8 multiple surgeries and lead to me being disabled. The rehabilitation for these surgeries would take years. Meanwhile I was pumped full with pain medications and nothing would ever stop the pain. The chronic pain was unbearable. The pain of no cartilage in a joint, bone rubbing against bone, or against a metal plate, or screws every time you turned your wrist is indescribable. Sometimes the pain was so great I would just look at my wrist and expect it to look injured or deformed because it hurt so bad. I would talk to my wrist like, "Why are you hurting just resting on my leg!" By January of 2016 I had reached a place in my life where I had given up. I didn't want to kill myself, but I didn't want to be here anymore. Every night I went to bed and I prayed I wouldn't wake up. I didn't feel that I had any purpose. I didn't believe I had any value. I couldn't physically do the things I did before. My life consisted of lying in the bed or lying on the sofa. I was the heaviest I had ever been, and in the darkest place I had ever felt. Though I knew my husband loved me, I longed for him to have a better life than I was able to give him. The reality of when a person gives up on life, their body will begin to die is so true. The power of our mind can be positive to our bodies or it can be negative and the affects are detrimental.

April 21, 2016, the pain I felt was gut wrenching. I realized Prince had become a part of my soul and the loss I was feeling was deep and real, even though I had never had a conversation with the man. I was forced to re-examine my life. My life had taken a full 360. I was forced to make hard decisions and move into a place of un-comfortableness that I had not been to in years.

I went to Minneapolis in September 2016 to see *The Revolution* at First Avenue for their tribute concert to Prince. It felt as though we were going to a memorial service as we drove to First Avenue that day. The night was unbelievable. It was a rollercoaster of emotions. Crying. Hugging. Laughing. Excitement. Celebrating. More crying, times of people wailing crying and then times of jumping and singing! It was like Prince was there and would be coming on the stage at any moment; and we were all just watching and waiting for him to say, "Surprise!" It felt like he was there. Those two nights the devastation of loss from the fams; or family as Prince called us, was the most undeniable sight of pain I had ever seen in a group of 1,500 people gathered together under one roof. You could see the pain and you could feel it. It was pure extreme grief. You could feel him everywhere.

The difference at the Official Tribute in October 2016 wasn't because we didn't still feel all the same emotions those that were at the First Avenue experienced, the difference was Morris Hayes and what he had put together for us, the purple family, in such a short time. Morris had as many of Prince's entourage of band members, close friends, elite artists in music recording industry from his beginning to the end and some that Prince simply loved and respected as musicians. Not only was it a night of incredible, amazing, mind-blowing music, dancing and choreography, it was of course an area full of the Purple World in rare form showing our love for Prince in every shape and form by dressing in character, color and design. But, I must say above all, what tore my heart the deepest was the love shown on the stage by almost every person who performed and gave their performance back to "Prince" with a pointed finger to heaven asking us all not to give applause to them, but to Prince. That showed true love, true respect and what I believed exactly what Prince deserved. It was Magnificent! Thank you Morris Hayes and all that participated in the Official Tribute should know you did Prince proud and we appreciated the opportunity to share that night with you all. Shout out, great love and respect "Mr. Hayes" for making sure Prince was given a Tribute we as the purple family think he would've approved of. Music was his life and we enjoyed 5 hours of history that night with "our purple world family".

Minnesota is a beautiful state but after going there and meeting the people talk about Prince and hear the stories, there is something that is so special there. You get why he stayed there and didn't leave, and it's not just because, "It gets so cold it keeps the bad people out" as he would say. As soon as I stood at the fence at Paisley Park I felt peace. The fence was covered in tributes, and mementos from hundreds of purple fams who came from all around the world to show their immense love and respect for Prince. It was a shrine and it was something to witness! I wish it could have lasted forever! Please look it up online and see with your own eyes a picture of the tremendous love shown for this man. One of the greatest things that happened when we were at "that Paisley Park fence", we met some of the most incredible people from other countries, other states, different races, and different walks of life. We are all different until we come to "the fence" and we become the group of people who do not see religion, race or creed. We unite together in complete love and understanding for one another that Prince has touched each one of our lives in a way so deeply that we had to get in a car and drive thousands of miles, or hop on a plane and fly to Minnesota, just to stand by "the fence" and pay our respects. The love was overwhelming. I didn't want to leave. We met people from South Korea, Bosnia, New York, Japan, California, Chicago, Norway, the United Kingdom, Minnesota, China, Denmark, Australia, Texas, New Jersey, Ohio and many other cities. I have stayed connected with several people we met on our first visit who have since become very close friends. We went back to "the fence" daily, while we were there, and it was always the same – Magical! So if you're contemplating on whether or not you should visit Paisley Park, don't think about it, do it.

There is something you should know about when you go to Minneapolis, if you're a Prince person and you're dealing with his passing or even if you're going to show respect to him. When you leave there, something happens to you. It's another process. I have gone several times since he passed and each time I have had incredible, wonderful, experiences. The Official Tribute in October 2016 and the Official Opening of Paisley Park as a Museum, the One Year Anniversary 2017, His Birthday in June 2017, my 50th Birthday, and Super Bowl LII Weekend in 2018. But when you get home there is always something that hits you, and you have this feeling of wanting to be back there. There is something there that feels like home and you understand why Prince never left Minnesota. Paisley Park is in our hearts, just as he planned for it to be, like a home away from home. Where there's always a longing to go back and visit. I have been very fortunate to have made some lovely friends who have become family and have afforded me opportunities to visit more often. Because of this, these people have become some of the most important people in my life. I know they will be in my life for the rest of my life.

Each person was placed in my path at very specific moments and life-changing events have evolved from these encounters. None of these things wonderful things would have happened without the tragic loss of Prince.

An awakening happened and my life has not been the same. The jolt of the world's sudden loss of Prince was so profound that it caused me to wake up and start doing some really hard work in resolving deeply routed issues of my past. In doing the work, I was able to completely go back to all those times and places where Prince was instrumental in my life and actually deal with whatever it was and move on to the next issue. Ultimately I got to a place where all the things I had just buried away and not dealt with were pulled out, processed and no longer a part of my being. It enabled me to reach a place in my spirituality that allowed me to give complete trust to God in every aspect of my life. The freedom that came from being able to lay it all down and not pick up some pieces again has brought me to a place that I can only pray every person reaches in their lifetime. It is what true freedom feels like. Can you feel it? I want you to feel it, to know it, to experience it. You can, you just have to trust in Him and lay it all down and walk away not looking back.

So much love and peace has come to me from going to Paisley Park and meeting some of the most incredible people. From ordinary people that live around the world becoming friends and family to some of Prince's closest inner circle, I have moved from a place of despair to a place of complete peace and trust in my Lord and Savior Jesus Christ. I know that I had only gotten to this place because of the constants in my life. Prince's presence from early on and carrying me for all those years in my mind and in my soul, Reed; my God-Father who showed me what an honorable Father was, Jesus Christ; who saved me and gave me complete freedom and Ron; my husband who has stood by my side through thick and thin, sickness and health, and when I did everything I could to push him away he pushed and prayed for me, never against me. Without those constants I would never have made it to the place I am today. I go to bed thanking God for the day to come, eager and excited to see how He will use me in His kingdom. It is a beautiful thing.

I have a new beginning, a fresh opportunity in this thing called life. I would encourage you to research Prince if you don't know him. Listen to his music, not just Purple Rain because he is so much more than that album. He is a genius, a self-taught musician that produced, engineered, wrote, sang and played every instrument on his first album. How many artist do you know who can say they did that and did it well? Listen to his jazz songs, learn what being "funky" really is cause if I have to explain it you don't know it! Pay attention to Real Music by Real

Musicians. There is a difference. Look up his discography and listen to an album you never heard before, order a book and learn about an era of time that you are not so familiar with, just get to know the man himself. The easiest way to do that is to listen to the music and read the words to the lyrics. He has never had a problem being very clear in saying what he wanted us to hear. We need to open our ears to hear what he was saying. Music was his life. Learn it. This man stood for many things. He taught us many things. Find something that he teaches you and teach it to someone else. We must respect his legacy and continue spreading his message. Find your foundation and stand on it. Spread love and never hate. Make a difference with your life.

Love 4 one another – I've seen and felt the true meaning of this in many arms of the purple family. I look at Prince's life, how he gave, the lives he changed and I'm in awe of the LOVE he was a part of creating in a world of diverse races and religions. I look at him and I pray that in my lifetime I can change just one life. I believe I will. He taught me that. I had forgotten until now.

How do you love someone you never knew? How do you say thank you when their time on earth is through? I don't know…… I just do. Thank you Prince.

Tia Weber Stasko, Louisiana

CONCLUSION

On April 21, 2016 I sat in my living room, watching the world light up in Purple. Little did I know the world had been purple for over 30 years. The past year I have had the privilege of experiencing some amazing moments. I was able to see the amazing Sheila E. play her heart out. I got to see her holding back tears while she sang her song that she had written for her friend and companion Prince. I got to witness the unity of the Purple Family while waiting in line to see The Revolution. Everyone telling their stories and talking about previous Prince shows they had seen. To hearing The Revolution play *Sometimes It Snows In April* and seeing tears rundown everyone's faces. My sweet daughter was able to dance with Mayte Garcia, thanks to The Paisley 5 & Dime. Everyone there welcomed us with open arms, and we have memories from that experience to last a life time. My life has become so much richer thanks to Prince. The people I have met, and the experiences I have had changed my life.

Nine months ago, I had a dream about Prince. We were dancing like old friends. He looked so healthy, his hair was long and was wearing a light-yellow jumpsuit. We were laughing and I gave him a hug (even in my dreams I had to slightly bind down due to his small stature). I told him, "The world knows the good that you have done and we are all so proud of you." He pulled back with tears in his eyes and gave me a shy smile. I then woke up. I laid in bed with a heavy heart. I knew that would be the last time I dreamt of him, and it was. Little did Prince know that by writing music, he was writing the story to so many people's lives. He is no longer physically with us, but his stories, philanthropy and music are still alive through us. If I could say one thing to Prince it would be, thank you. Thank you for the music. Thank you for your kindness. And most of all, thank you for the stories.

Printed in the United States
By Bookmasters